MOUNTAIN
BIKING for kids
Mindset Development Guide

Mountain Biking For Kids:

MINDSET DEVELOPMENT GUIDE

Christopher C. Keller

COPYRIGHT

***Mountain Biking* For Kids:**

By Christopher C. Keller

MOUNTAIN
BIKING for Kids
Mindset Development Guide
Christopher C. Keller

TABLE OF CONTENTS

INTRODUCTION:

Welcome to the first edition of Developing Mountain Biking Skills for Kids. Just like the season's changes, Mountain Biking skills are changing. To become a good Mountain Biker, the secret is developing your skills regularly.

This edition of Developing Mountain Biking Skills will introduce you to the world of Mountain Biking. It also focuses on how to select the right bike and how to develop your mountain biking skills.

For those with a bike riding skill, this edition of mountain biking will help you become a better rider and improve your knowledge about mountain biking.

I learnt about mountain biking at the age of 6, and by the age of 15, I have toured most of the trails in Colorado. The first step to becoming a great mountain biker is understanding that you can become better- whether young, old, timid beginner and professionals.

Why You Need This Guide?

Everybody needs a guide to becoming successful. Even soccer players need coaches to win trophies. Also, in mountain biking, we need guides and to be guided to become better riders.

By having this guide, you will be able to:

- Improve your mountain biking skills faster and build confidence quickly.

- Get corrections and learn from your mistakes which will help you become better.

- Learn from the experiences of a Great Mountain Biker.

- Build a better relationship with your bike and increase your love for the sport.

DISCLAIMER

Mountain biking can be dangerous just like any other sport. You can hurt yourself or destroy your bike. These are some of the reason why it is an exciting sport. Before riding a bike always remember to wear your protective gear. Also, remember not to perform skills you are yet to perfect to avoid injuries.

If you are riding on a rough trail, remember to wear your elbow and knee pad. Wear eye protection equipment to prevent dust or dirt from entering your eyes. Riding safely is the key to becoming a better rider and preventing injuries.

Welcome to the exciting world of Mountain Biking. Becoming a professional mountain biker takes time and practice. Remember to take it one step at a time!

CHAPTER ONE: WHAT IS MOUNTAIN BIKING?

Mountain Biking is a type of sport that involves riding bicycles off-road and over rough grounds, using specially created and designed mountain bikes. When we ride our bikes over rough areas especially around mountain trails, we are doing mountain biking. Remember, mountain bikes are different from the normal bicycles we ride to the shopping mall, to see a friend, or in our neighborhood.

What is a Mountain Bike?

A Mountain Bike is a type of bike that is designed for riding over rough areas such as stony ground, through the woods, and under rugged conditions. A mountain bike can take a lot of stress and abuse and still allow the rider to comfortably ride on rough terrain and go over or through obstacles that he or she may experience on the trail.

Parts of a Mountain Bike

The mountain bike consists of several parts that make it solid and great for rough riding. They include;

- ***TIRES***

The tires are usually wider and knobbier, which provides better grip and stability. Most tires have inflated tubes/interior inside, but there are newer variations also which features a tubeless tire system.

- ***HANDLEBAR***

The mountain bike handlebar is located at the front of the bike; this is what you used to steer or maneuver your bike. It also comes in different styles and shapes to meet the specific needs of any rider.

- ***FRAME***

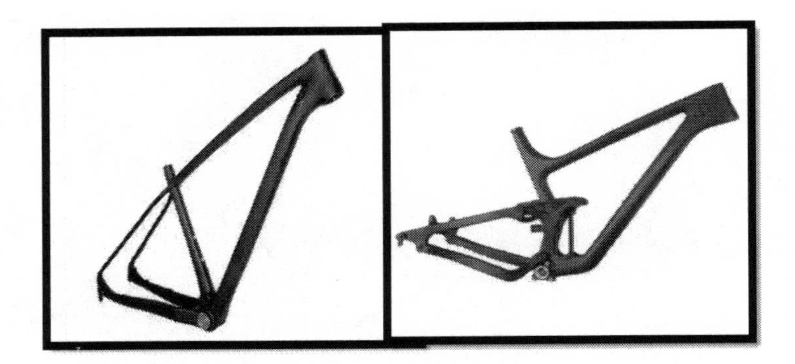

The mountain bike frame is the foundation/skeleton/core of the bike. This is responsible for holding the other entire mountain bike parts, whether they are the basic parts or bike accessories. It is essential that you decide the right frame size that matches your height and inseam to reward yourself a comfortable ride. The mountain bike frames also come in different materials according to their price and lightness – steel, alloy, aluminum, carbon fiber and the best of all is titanium material.

- ***Saddle***

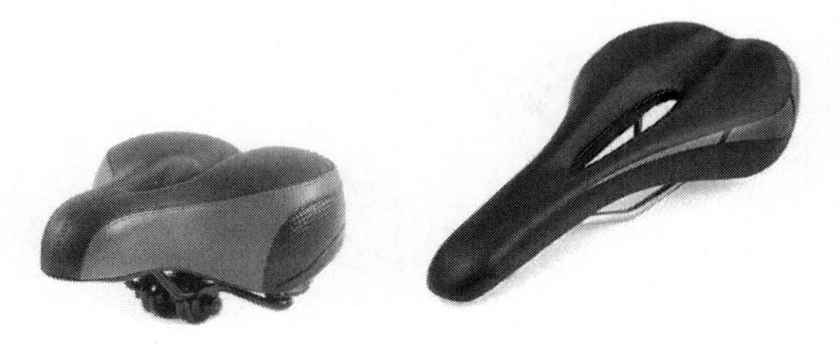

The mountain bike saddle help improves the comfort of your ride. Without a standard measured saddle that will catch your entire butt, then surely a pain on the road will be encountered. Take note also that more padding does not mean more comfort; it still depends on how you adjust your seat properly.

- ***PEDALS***

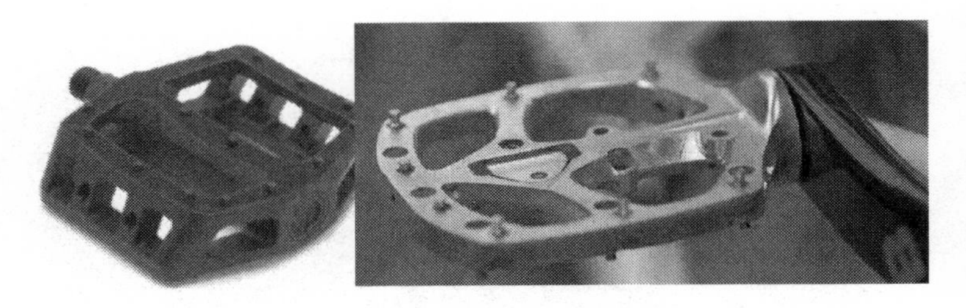

The pedals are where you step your two foot to create a cycled motion that will make the bike move. Choosing the right pedals will make you a better rider, make your ride safer, gives you more control with your bike and provides more pedaling efficiency.

The four basic type of pedals is basic platform, advanced platform, toe clips or cage style and clipless. There is also a newer type of pedals, which features a dual platform such as basic platform on one side and the other side is cage style.

- ***BRAKES***

Mountain bike brakes are a significant part of the bike because of its primary purpose to stop the bike. Aside from that, they also help regulate the speed, control your bike and make it possible to perform advanced techniques.

The two basic types of brakes are the disc brakes and the rim brakes. Disc brakes perform best even on muddy situations, but they are usually heavier than rim brakes.

BUYING THE RIGHT BIKE

While growing up, my beloved Father was a seasoned Mountain Biker. He and his friends every weekend toured the mountain trails of Colorado. The sight of them with their shiny and colorfully designed mountain bikes ignited my love for mountain biking.

Lo and behold, at the age of 14, my Father gifted me a cheap carbon fiber Kestrel 200SC which he bought for $130. I was super excited because I was now among the kids in my neighborhood with a Mountain Bike. Every weekend, I toured the nearby woods with my pals, Brian and Clair. We would ride for hours until we were tired and return home to rest. Every time we rode, I noticed that my bike lacked traction or friction which made me crash frequently. One time, the handlebar came off suddenly which left me injured for a week.

It lasted about three months before I wrecked it trying to downhill a virgin path off the side of a mountain along the Emerald Lake trail. The front brake broke first, then the chain snapped, and finally, the right pedal came off. So, don't buy cheap, and buy what you need.

Buying the right bike is very important because it saves you from spending much on repairs, saves you from frequent injuries, and allows you to go over a rough surface easily. There are quite a lot of mountain bikes available on the market today. From kid-sized bikes to adult bikes.

TYPES OF MOUNTAIN BIKES

Mountain bikes are designed in various ways to suit specific riding style and environment. Most of the time, the differences are usually seen in the different suspension design, body frame, handlebar design, and the tire types.

With several bikes available in the market at different prices, choosing a specific bike can be a hard decision especially if you are a beginner.

Below are the two basic types of Mountain bikes available in the market for both kids and adults.

Cross Country Mountain Bikes

Cross-country bikes are the most common bikes available in the market and are also referred to as XC bikes. These types of bikes are usually light in weight and designed for speed purposes. Most of the times, they are sold for between $200- $1000. The XC bikes available in the market are usually of two basic types, namely; The XC Race bike and the XC Trail bike.

The XC Race bikes are usually lightweight, fast and great for riding over rough terrain. The only disadvantage of the XC Race bikes is that they are not a great option for performing high jumping and landing.

The XC Trail bikes are the go-to mountain bike for all forms of mountain biking. While the XC Trail bikes are slightly heavier than the XC Racers, they are excellent for both dirt road and single-track trail riding. Most of the mountain bikes available in the market today are of the XC Trail category.

All Mountain/Enduro Mountain Bikes

This is one of the most popular types of mountain bikes in the world today. All mountain or the Enduro mountain bike share quite a lot of similarities with the XC Trail bike. The differences between the two bikes are that the All Mountain bikes offer a stronger frame and allow for more travel in the suspension (around 140-160mm).

The reason for the allowance of more travel in the suspension is to allow the rider to go over more difficult trail obstacles. The All Mountain bikes also feature a wider tire to allow for extra grip and traction which sets it apart from the XC Trail bikes. If you are a beginner confused about which type of bike you need, then this is an excellent choice.

What Should You Look Out for Before Buying a Kid's Mountain Bike?

After my experience with my crashed Kestrel 200C, I decided to purchase a new mountain bike after saving my money all through the year. At this point, I was a little boy at the age of 15 with a tiny body frame. I wanted a long-lasting bike that can serve all my mountain biking purposes.

To be able to buy the right bike, I started studying about bikes, read magazines such as the Mountain & the City Biking. This helped me learn a lot before purchasing my new mountain bike. Purchasing the right kid mountain bike is very important because it saves you money and makes riding fun.

Below are five (5) things you should look out for before buying a kid's mountain bike;

It should fit properly

When buying a kid mountain bike, it should fit properly. That is, you should be able to straddle the bike with both feet touching the ground. Also, when seating on the saddle, your feet should be able to touch the ground with ease.

Buying a bike that fits properly is important because it allows for ease of use and safety. A mountain bike that doesn't allow you to reach the handlebar or brakes while seated is very dangerous. As parents, endeavor to buy a mountain bike that suits your kids present weight and height and not one he/she will grow into.

Physical/Mountain Biking Experience

Before buying a mountain bike, first, determine the biking experience of your child/children. While there are several mountain bikes available for certain ages, the physical ability or biking experience of your child matters a lot.

At the age of 6, some children may be able to balance, steer, and pedal effectively while others may not be able to do the same at the same age.

The Weight of the Bike

The weight of the bike is also of great importance. My first mountain bike which was gifted to me by my father was about 20 inch in length and quite heavy. Every time I went biking, I always struggled to control the bike which led to many crashes.

When you are considering buying a kid mountain bike, you should consider the ratio of the bike's weight with your weight. It is advisable that you should buy a mountain bike that is one-half of your weight. Remember that kids are not as strong adults so the lighter the bike, the better.

Look Out for The Number of Gears

For beginners or those who hope to do most of their riding within their neighborhoods, single speed bikes are great! This is because Single speed bikes are easier to manage, lighter, and less likely to need repairs.

Once you start to ride on a trail with much climbing and descending, gears can increase the fun and reduce the work of climbing up hills. Today, it is now possible to see kids' bikes with up to 27 gears which are both confusing and heavy for kids.

In our opinion, a 1x with 7-9 gears is enough to give your kid the range to make it up steep hills and still pick up some speed when its flat.

Learn about the Right Suspension Option

Suspensions are important parts of a bike. They allow for a smooth riding experience which is important. Most of the suspension found on kid-sized bikes are usually cheap and ineffective. This is because kids do not possess enough body mass to compress a front shock.

Although most kid and parents in general usually prefer a mountain bike with a front shock, it is advisable to go with a mountain bike that features a rigid fork.

Health Benefits of Mountain Biking

Mountain biking is a great sport because it helps in keeping our body healthy. Just like every other sport, mountain biking helps us stay healthy and far from illness. Apart from the fun mountain biking gives us, it gives us physical benefits.

Below are (5) five reasons why we should engage in mountain biking;

- It reduces diseases: Mountain biking helps in preventing diseases. Although, we might experience some bruises from riding, biking for three hours weekly is all we need to prevent overweight or reduce body fat.

- It decreases stress: Mountain biking is a great way to reduce stress. This is because it makes you happy which is important in reducing stress.

- Mountain Biking helps you meet to meet new friends: Mountain biking is a great way to meet new people from different places. Being part of a biking club is a great way to make new friends and learn new skills.

- It helps in boosting self-confidence: Growing up I was a timid kid who was usually bullied because of my tiny body size. Engaging in mountain biking helped me gain my self-confidence. It helped me build my physical appearance and every trail I completed made me feel like a hero.

- It is a Source of Fun: Biking through a mountain trail or paved trail with friends and family members is one of the best types of outdoor fun. The joy of getting to meet new friends, sing war songs and school rhymes together while riding makes mountain biking a great source of fun.

CONCLUSION

This chapter was more of an introduction to the world of mountain biking. We have been able to cover the meaning of mountain biking, mountain bike, health benefits of mountain biking and types of mountain bikes.

Also, we believe that you now have an idea on what to look out for when buying your next mountain bike and the various parts of a mountain bike. Read the next chapter to learn more about developing your mountain biking skills.

CHAPTER TWO

In chapter one, we talked about the meaning of mountain biking and mountain bike, the various types of mountain bikes, parts of a mountain bike, and the health benefits of mountain biking.

In this chapter, we will be discussing the various steps of learning how to ride a mountain bike. This chapter will cover areas such as understanding your bike, learning how to mount and unmount the right way, pedaling like a pro, and how to balance. The goal of this chapter is to help you build the necessary confidence and knowledge needed to start riding a mountain bike.

GETTING INTO THE RIGHT POSTURE

When it comes to mountain biking successfully, learning how to position your body is the secret to biking correctly. Mountain bike trails usually consist of stones, roots, mud or sand.

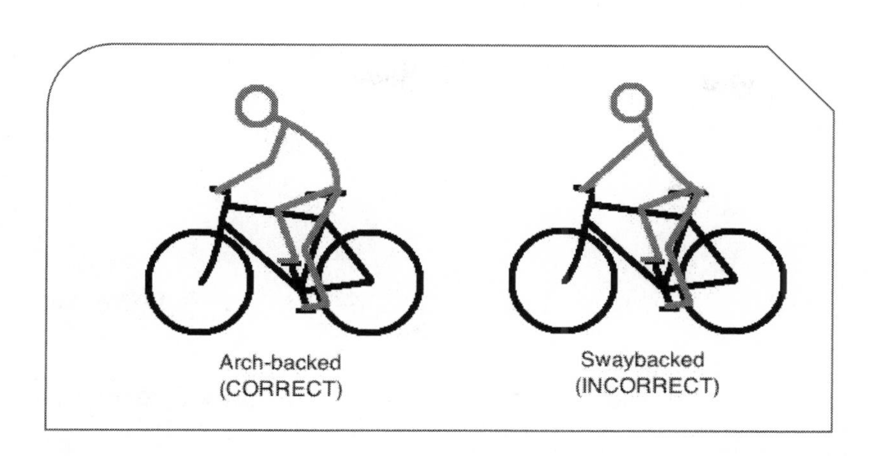

Although the roughness of the terrains is usually a source of additional fun, this can be a thing of worry for beginners especially kids. Learning how to position your body is the first step to becoming a better rider.

Also, having the right body position can help you get pass rockier and trick areas of the trail. There are two basic body positions; Neutral body position and Ready or Attack body position.

HOW TO GET INTO NEUTRAL POSITION WITH YOUR BIKE

When riding over a plain or flat terrain or trail such as your neighborhood trail, field, and dirt road you should be in the neutral position. Getting into a neutral position is quite easy. To ride in the neutral position, your knees and elbows should be slightly bent, index fingers on the brakes, and eyes looking around 20 feet ahead of you.

How to Get into Attack Position with your Bike

The attack or ready position is excellent for riding over rocky or steep terrain. When the trail gets steeper and rockier, it is time to get into the attack position. The Ready Position is used when mountain biking through difficult terrain.

This position is used to survive the roughness of the trail or when expecting rockier path ahead. It is also used in the practice of challenging skills or when trying to maneuver or take a corner during biking. Although, the Neutral and Ready positions are almost the same, to achieve the ready position;

- Level pedals that are evenly weighted
- A deep bend in the knees and elbows (think of making chicken wings with your arms with a 90-degree bend.)
- Take your buttocks off the seat and hips shifted back

- Your back is flat and nearly parallel to the ground

- Index fingers on the brake levers 100% of the time (rim brakes often require two fingers)

- Eyes forward-looking about 15 to 20 ft. ahead; look where you want to go, not where you don't

- Your mind is confident and attentive.

Learning the Balance Strategy

Balance is one of the most important aspects of mountain biking. Like my father will always say to me when I started mountain biking, 'son, you can only become a better rider when you balance better'.

When your balancing skill is in top form, it allows you to ride comfortably and efficiently. Most new or even professional riders fail to understand the importance of proper balancing. Balancing properly makes riding your bike easy and more fun.

To build a better balance, it is best done when you are biking. So, after reading through this book, get on your bike and start practicing.

Below are various exercise tips from **Dean Golich**, a former Psychologist for the USA Cycling team that has helped many become better at balancing.

- ***THE QUICK WARM UP***

Before you begin biking, take a few minutes to move around the cockpit area. Move your weight back as far as you can, above the rear wheel, then move your weight forward, then to the sides, then low on the bike. By doing these exercises, you'll be more comfortable doing them when you are biking.

- ***LEARN TO RIDE SLOWLY***

Ride as slowly as you possibly can--get right to that "I'm going to topple over" point and focus on moving around to stay upright. When you're comfortable with this, pick a line (a piece of curbing in the parking lot, a log or board on the trail) and ride along it, as slowly as possible. Then do it again, and go even slower.

- ***STAND STILL***

When you stop on the trail (to wait for your buddies and take a breather), don't put a foot down. Instead, practice your track stand--stay upright and still, keeping the pressure on the pedals with the brakes applied to control movement. Hint: all these drills are more comfortable with flat pedals.

MOUNTING AND DISMOUNTING

While mounting and dismounting your bike might sound easy, there is still the need to develop a proper and quicker technique. Being able to mount and dismount your bike will make you not only a safer rider but also an efficient rider. This is important when the time is of the essence especially during bike races.

Mounting Techniques

- When mounting or climbing your bike, it is advisable to mount your bike from the left side of the bike. Mounting your bike from the left helps to prevent you from getting stained by your chain oil. Also, in places like the UK, it is a safety rule that cyclist mounts their bikes from the left side.

- Stand beside the bike with both hands holding the handlebars. Lift your right leg over the back of the saddle and place your right foot onto the pedal. Bring the right pedal up to the two o'clock position. If you can, slide your backside onto the saddle. You may only be touching the floor with the ball of your left foot, but that's fine, it's just there for initial balance.

- Look behind you to check that there's no approaching traffic. If all is clear now, then look ahead to where you want to steer, push down with your right foot to begin pedaling and push off with your left foot then bring your backside onto the saddle (if it's not already there). As the left pedal comes around, place your left foot on the pedal and continue pedaling.

Dismounting Techniques

When riding through a specific trail or off the road, it is quite common to come across obstacles such as big rocks, very rough surfaces that you may not be able to ride through. The best thing to do is to alight or dismount smoothly and continue on foot before remounting your bike.

Dismounting your mountain bike is quite easy especially when it is your size or adjusted to suit your size. One of the problems faced by many bikers is the issue of their saddle being too high. If your saddle is too high, you may experience a problem getting off it easily.

Also, always check if your brakes are working properly before the start of any biking activities. Below are several ways you can dismount your mountain bikes faster and comfortably.

- Begin to brake as you approach the obstacle; do so well in advance so that you do not have to panic. Use both brakes equally, unless it is downhill, in which case use the front brake very lightly. If you are heading uphill, gravity will slow you, so you needn't worry too much about braking.

- Whether you are left or right handed it is always best to get off the left side of the bike. This avoids you getting covered in oil from the chain and gears.

- Once parked, place your left foot on the floor. You will probably need to lean the bike slightly to the left (if the bike is set up properly you will only be able to touch the ground with the bottom of one foot when seated on the saddle).

- Move off the saddle to place your left foot flat on the ground and then take your right foot off the pedal and bring your right leg around and over the back of the saddle so that you are standing with the bike on your right.

LEARNING HOW TO CONTROL YOUR SPEED

When it comes to mountain biking, everyone wants to ride fast or go faster than his or her normal speed. Either going through a smooth trail or going over an obstacle, there is always an urge to go over in speed. However, being unable to control your speed may lead you to frequent accident and destruction of your bike.

While growing up, I was always attracted to fast things- fast cars, fast bikes, fast athletes until I got my bike. One day, my friend Josh and I embarked on a wood trail with the first to get to the other end of the wood winning a chocolate cookie. Josh was a better rider than I, but I was determined to defeat him.

As the race started, Josh took off with high speed, cutting through corners, and dodging trees. I followed suit but little did I know that there was a log of tree trunk lying on the dirt road. Before I could notice the obstacle, I was already close and lost control of my bike. The result was a broken handlebar, punctured tire and bruised arm.

Being able to control your speed is one of the most important aspects of mountain biking. Below are several ways you can learn how to control your speed even as a beginner.

- ***Develop a Focused Mind***

There is always that urge within every rider to break the speed or ask themselves the question, am I riding too fast? It is an unconscious habit to be in control of your bike when you feel you are riding too fast. Yielding to this thought all the time will prevent you from exploring your speed limit.

So, before you brake, learn to look ahead to see if you can find another way out without breaking your speed.

- ***LEARN HOW TO BRAKE WITH FORCE***

Being able to press the brake with confidence is the first step to being able to ride through any trail or turn with great speed. To be able to brake with confidence, start by doing the following things;

- Compress your bike suspension and tires for maximum friction or traction.
- Drop your center of gravity as your body pushes into the bike
- Use the maximum braking force before your tires lock.

- ***STAY OFF THE BRAKES WHEN IN A TURN***

When in a turn, it is best when you lean your bike into a turn instead of grabbing the brakes. If you go for the brakes when in a turn, it will cause your bike to be more uptight which may make you lose control of your bike. This is why many riders feel like they can't hold some turns – it's caused by them dabbing the brakes part way through.

To break the habit, find a good corner and practice on breaking hard when approaching then ride through at a steady pace without going for the brakes.

PEDALING LIKE A PROFESSIONAL

Pedaling like a professional as a kid is quite easy if practiced regularly. Professional cyclist or mountain bikers that rider excellently has just two things going for them. They are; A knowledge of how to pedal properly and a bike that properly fits their body size.

To be able to understand how to pedal like a professional, it involves using some techniques shared by my friend, Paulo Sadhana, a Professional Physiologist;

- The ball of the foot – that's the padded portion of the sole between the toes and the arch – should rest on the surface of the pedal. The feet should be pointing straight forward.

- The first part of the pedal stroke begins at the 11 o'clock position. From there, you should push forward onto the pedal until they reach the 1 o'clock position.

- Once the foot reaches the 1 o'clock position, you should feel yourself pushing down on the pedal with the full power of their leg until the 5 o'clock position. This is the phase of the stroke where most of the power is generated.

- From the 5 o'clock to the 7 o'clock position, you should focus on pointing the foot downward. This will build the good habit of "pulling the pedal" when they get older and transition to wearing cycling shoes for mountain or road biking.

- Once they reach the 7 o'clock position, the focus should be for you to keep light pressure on the pedal during this phase, because the opposite leg will be working to help turn the pedals.

Conclusion

This chapter has been able to reveal the various secrets behind getting into the various body positions, balance strategy, how to dismount and mount your mountain bike the right way. Also, we have been able to learn a few things about controlling your speed and how to pedal like a pro. Remember that becoming a great cyclist or mountain biker is only because of constant practice and dedication.

CHAPTER THREE: SADDLE CHOICE AND FIT

Choosing a saddle can be a challenge, but it's worth putting the effort in to find the right one for you, and the key thing to look for is comfort — the more comfortable you are, the longer (and faster) you'll be able to ride.

Unfortunately, saddle comfort is based on personal opinions. Ask a dozen riders what the most comfortable saddle is, and you'll get a dozen answers.

This isn't surprising. When you sit on a bike, your weight rests on a pair of bones collectively called the ischial tuberosity or, more familiarly, the sit bones. These are positioned differently on different riders.

Not only that but depending on your riding style and bike set-up, you'll experience pressure on different areas to the next rider.

When I bought my first real mountain bike in 1998, it came with a sweet saddle—or so I thought. It was a Selle Italia with custom maple leaf corners to match the signature maple leaves painted on the frame of my new Rocky Mountain Oxygen Race.

Selle Italia is a respected name in saddles with a full line, and 14 years ago, $850 was much money to drop on a hardtail, so I figured all was good to go. Not so. That thing *hurt*, especially for any ride longer than about an hour. I figured. It was all my fault—new rider, poor technique, etc. Again, not so as I proved when I replaced it with a new WTB saddle that was the perfect fit for me.

WHAT ARE THE PARTS OF A MOUNTAIN BIKE SADDLE?

The basic part of a mountain bike saddle may be divided into four parts:

- ***SHELL:***

The Shells are generally some hard plastic, but carbon fiber is becoming more popular.

- ***PADDING:***

The Padding is the squishy part between the shell and the cover; padding thicknesses can be of different level or amount.

- ***Cover:***

Covers may be all leather, synthetic material, or some combination of leather with reinforced Kevlar corners.

- ***Rails:***

Rails are usually made of alloy, with pure titanium occupying the higher end of the performance.

Saddle Shape and Fit

Deciding on your required features and level of performance is the easy part. Getting the best fit may be a little more challenging. The basic saddle shape can be important. As we previously discussed, a broad, chair-like saddle would be most comfortable, but these are usually limited to comfort bikes and rarely appear on mountain bikes.

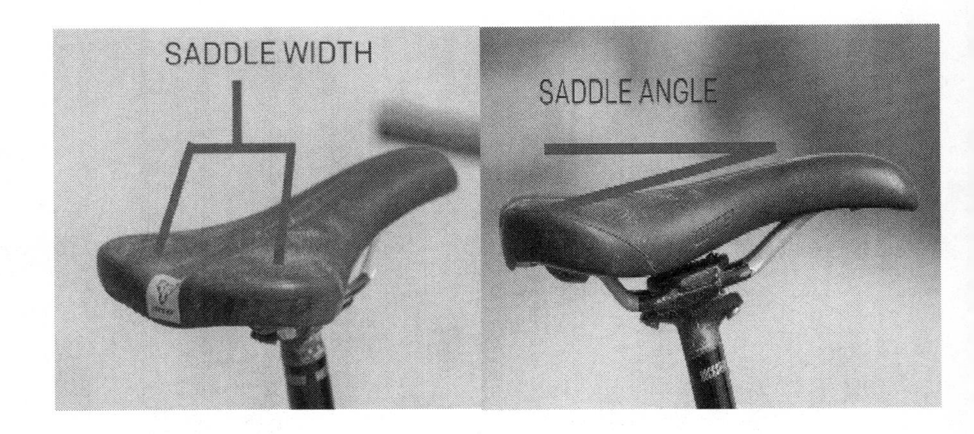

Instead, long, thin saddles have real applicability on the trails. For the racers, the narrow profile, in addition to saving weight, also allows for a more comfortable, more efficient pedaling.

Can I try before I buy?

Well, sometimes, a few manufacturers provide dealers with demo saddles. Check with your local bike shop to see if this is the case for any of the lines they carry. If not, you're going to have to do your best just by trying other bikes.

Take a test ride on a bike, demo a bike, borrow your buddy's bike. Find what shape and style are comfortable for you and then try to buy either that same saddle or one built and shaped like it.

SUSPENSION CHOICE AND SETUP

Getting a new mountain bike is exciting. However, choosing and setting up your MTB suspension properly is important. One of the reasons is that it helps you to get the best out of your mountain bike as a proper bike fit. You are better off with a good bike with well set-up suspension than a good bike with poorly set-up suspension.

Modern mountain bikes are nearly all equipped with suspension. The purpose of suspension is to reduce the roughness of the terrain, providing the rider with a smoother, more controlled ride.

A bike with just **front suspension (a suspension fork) is referred to as a hardtail**, a bike with **both front and rear suspension is referred to as a dual-suspension**, or full-suspension bike and a **bike without any suspension at all are known as a rigid mountain bike.**

In other words, MTB suspension is important. Here are some parts of a mountain bike suspension system.

- ***Fork***

Forks are also known as front suspension or front shocks. There are many options and brands available and, are easy to change out assuming you have a compatible travel length and wheel size.

- ***Shocks***

These are joined to the suspension frames and are also known as rear shocks. Size, stroke length, and damper tunes are built specially for different frames. These are much less interchangeable and in some cases are proprietary to the frame and cannot be changed.

- ***Spring and Damper***

All mountain bike suspension, whether a fork or rear shock has two main functions which are performed by the spring and the damper. The spring primarily provides **resistance** while the damper provides the **control of that resistance**. There are two types of springs: air and coil.

- ***Air Springs***

Air springs are more and more common on mountain bikes, from bikes for beginners to advanced bikes. The advantage with air springs is their light weight and tune-ability. With a shock pump, you can set the air spring resistance to exactly what you're looking for on the fly.

Air spring volume, which further changes the kinematics of the shock, can be adjusted on some bike models. The disadvantage is that in some cases, they don't (generally speaking) provide quite the response and performance of coil springs.

- ***Coil Springs***

Exactly what it sounds like! A metal corkscrew coil is what provides the resistance. The same mechanism that's in your clicky-pen is also what helps you safely case that gap jump you come up short on. These are usually made from steel, but fancier shocks can have titanium springs as well.

The main disadvantage is that the weight of coil shocks can be heavier than the air springs and have less adjustment range, but they can provide a trail feeling that's so sensitive; you may wonder if you have a flat tire.

GEAR SELECTION

Whether you ride a mountain bike, a road bike or a commuter bike - in fact, pretty much any bike - you'll have gears. They are the mechanical wonders that will allow you to accelerate to the wind whistling speed along smooth flat roads or power your way up a steep rocky climb without losing your speed or balance.

Understanding your bike gears is simple. You push the lever one way to make it easier to pedal, and the other to go faster. Choosing the right gears to install on your bike, however, can be much trickier.

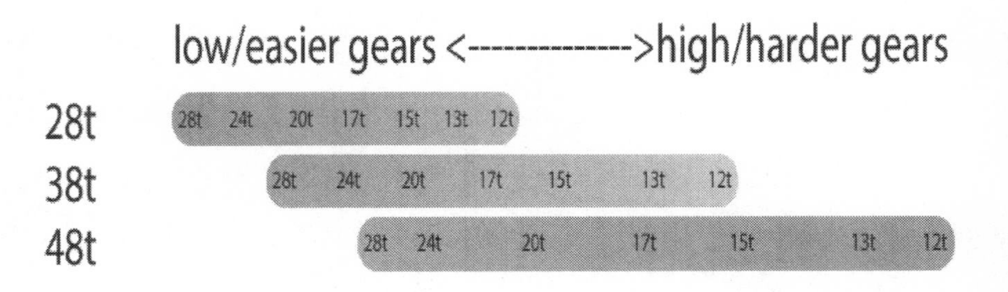

Most of us end up riding the gears that came with our bikes, but if you don't think about swapping out for different scenarios, you might end up making things much more difficult than they need to be.

The gear ratios you want to use for a hilly cycling holiday in London are not the same as the gears you want for a time trial, club ride or city riding. Our complete guide to bike gears takes the difficulty out and will have you joining in with all the other boys/girls talking on about ratios in no time at all.

FRONT GEARS (CHAINRINGS/CRANKSET)

The front gears are referred to as chainrings, or as a crankset. The whole assembly with the crank arms and the front gears together is properly known as the 'crankset,' or sometimes 'chainset.' Most cranksets have either two (called a double or 2x) or three (called a triple or 3x) chainrings. Single (or 1x) chainrings are gaining popularity, particularly among mountain bikers.

Rear Gears (Cassettes)

The gears on the rear wheel are called **'cogs,'** and when you put a few of them together in ascending size and attach them onto your back wheel, they are referred to as a 'cassette.' Most bikes built in the last few years have between 8 and 11 cogs in the cassette.

The largest cogs are closest to the wheel, and the gears are numbered from the inside out. The larger the cog the 'lower' the gear and the easier it will be to pedal, but the slower you will go.

Derailleurs

Derailleur' is hard to pronounce, but easy to understand. The chain gets moved from one cog to another or one chainring to another using a derailleur. The front derailleur is a simple device that pushes the chain off one chainring to be picked up or 'caught' by the next.

The rear derailleur is a little more complex as it has two jobs. Like the front, it guides the chain from one cog to the next, but it is also responsible for maintaining chain tension and taking up the slack when we move from bigger gears to smaller ones.

Learn how to use your bike gears, and you'll be rewarded with a smooth, fast, and fun ride. These top tips will get you up to speed in no time. (Sorry, we couldn't resist!)

- ***Practice Makes Perfect***

You'll be using your bike gears a lot, and the chances are you'll get plenty of practice in as you ride anyway, but if you're new to mountain biking, have just got a new bike or changed bike, then spend some time getting used to how the gears change.

Ride up a down a quiet road or path and practice shifting up and down the gears, both front and back until you can change gear almost instinctively.

- ***Right = Rear, Left = Front***

Most bikes will have two sets of gear cogs. The front set, known as the chainrings, will give you big changes in gear. The front derailleur that shifts the chain between these chainrings is controlled by the left gear lever (or shifter).

The rear cogs (or sprockets) together form the cassette, and the derailleur that shifts the chain up and down these are controlled by the right shifter.

- ***Left = big changes, Right = fine tuning***

If you've got a hill coming up, it's quicker to shift down using the left shifter, which will shift the front gears, rather than the right which controls the rear gears. This will take you to an easier gear, and then you can fine tune using the rear gears.

- ***Anticipate the Obstacle***

When you are approaching a hill, get ready to start shifting down the gears as soon as the hill starts. That way, you won't be caught in too hard a gear halfway up, unable to pedal, which means you might have to get off and walk.

- ***DON'T SHIFT TOO QUICKLY***

If you are accelerating down a hill or on the flat, it's tempting to shift up to a higher gear as quickly as possible. On some bikes, this can cause the chain to jump off the gears completely, which means you'll have to stop and put it back on, which usually means greasy black fingers. Shift gradually, making sure the chain has engaged with each new gear before moving onto the next one.

SHIFTING AND CADENCE

The idea of shifting while cycling can seem confusing at first, but in a short time becomes familiar. Once you understand how shifting relates to cadence, you become more effective at using gears to ride faster and save energy. It's a win-win!

Understanding cadence is key to making good decisions with shifting. It is usually based on the calculation of how you are feeling, the slope of the road, the wind condition, and your fitness level.

Once you're able to understand how cadence and shifting work, you can reduce fatigue, ride for a longer period, and go faster with little effort. When Coaches say during training, **Spin to win**, this is exactly what they are talking about.

When it comes to shifting and cadence, there is a secret I learned when I started learning how to ride a mountain bike. The secret was for cadence, go for 85-100 RPM. This allows you to use less force per pedal stroke and easily adjust to changes. When climbing hills, it is better to go with 70-85 depending on the length and type of terrain.

Conclusion

This chapter was more of an advanced introduction to the world of mountain biking. We have been able to cover the suspension choice, saddle choice, shifting and cadence, and other important aspects.

Also, we believe that you now have an idea on what to look out for when buying these parts of a mountain bike. Read the next chapter to learn more about developing your mountain biking skills and how to stay safe.

CHAPTER FOUR: RIDING OVER OBSTACLES

One reason you bought a mountain bike is to take it off-road. However, off-road riding is nothing but a series of obstacles: sand, rocks, gravel, tree roots. Follow these tips and practice, practice, practice. Soon you'll be tackling your usual trails with confidence.

DROP-OFFS

A drop-off is a step down in a trail. The easiest drop-off is one that can be ridden at speed. Speed hop at the lip to prevent the front wheel from dropping.

If you're new to mountain biking, practice this from a curb, trying to get both wheels to contact the ground simultaneously.

- If a drop-off has to be taken slowly, push the handlebar in front of you as the wheel goes over the edge. The idea is to get the wheel to go over before you do.

- After the drop moves forward on the bike as soon as the steepness of the trail allows. The aim is to keep your weight over the balance point of the bike.

- If you stay way back on the bike, there isn't enough weight on the front tire to steer, and you're likely to crash on the next bump or stretch of sand.

➢ Sand

If you have a half-mile or more of sand to traverse, consider deflating your tires to gain traction; you'll "float" over the sand rather than cut through it. In general, it's best to stay seated when you hit a patch of sand.

- Shift your weight back a bit and try to pedal smoothly, maintaining even momentum.

- You want to keep your front wheel light, let it float a bit.

- Stay relaxed and try to steer with your body, not your handlebars.

➢ **Mud**

Mud presents one of the most difficult terrains, especially when combined with hills, rocks, logs, or roots.

- When you run into the mud, try to avoid sudden movements, use momentum as your friend.

- Steady pedal pressure and strength are required.

- Try to avoid braking, and approach obstacles as close to a 90-degree angle as possible.

If the mud is seriously deep or sticky, you probably shouldn't be riding the trail, anyway. Don't ride around a muddy portion of trail, if possible; you want to avoid widening the trail.

To maneuver a stretch of gravel,

- Keep your weight back and stay in the saddle.
- Pay attention to what's in front of you and work to maintain your balance. Avoid sudden movements, grip the handlebars firmly, go light on the front wheel
- Steer gradually by shifting your weight and not turning the handlebars.
- When cornering, keep the outside pedal at the bottom of the stroke and put some weight on it. This shifts your center of gravity as low as possible and helps with traction.

- **Roots**

- Approach a root at a 90-degree angle, speeding up slightly.
- Pull your front wheel up and over the root, and then lunge your upper body forward for added momentum to bring the rear wheel up and over.
- Be prepared for the rear tire to slide a bit. Several roots in a row require concentration, good balance and timing.

WATER BARS

Water bars are intentionally placed on some trails for erosion control, and it is best not to go around them as you create a funnel for the water.

- Slow down and ride them as you would a drop-off.
- As your bike handling skills progress, you might work toward "jumping" off the water bars, but doing so requires

not only clearing the water bar but maintaining control on the other side and perhaps preparing for the next water bar.

HOW TO JUMP A MOUNTAIN BIKE

The best way to learn how to jump on your mountain bike is to approach it with confidence, and proper protection will help provide that confidence.

Scouting the trail ahead of time is always a smart move, especially if your skills are still coming along or if it's your first time on a trail. Is that a tabletop or a gap? Be sure to scout the trail for jumps, so you know what's ahead. You don't want to ride up what you think is a tabletop that you can roll over only to find out at the last second that it's a gap.

After doing a scout, measure the jump. It can be helpful to pace out the distance of a jump from lip to lip before trying it. If you know you can successfully clear a gap that's ten heel-to-toe steps long on your home trail, then you can use that knowledge to inform your decision about trying a new jump.

Before attempting to do a jump, you must have mastered the following skills. These skills are important if you want to do a successful jump.

- **Skill one:** Learn to manual (lift the front wheel off the ground)
- **Skill two:** Learn to bunny hop (lift both wheels off the ground)
- **Skill three:** Combine a manual with a bunny hop while working on the three parts of a jump—the take-off, the air, and the landing.

Learn to Manual

There are two parts to the manual: getting the front wheel in the air and finding the balance point to keep it there. The key to both parts is using your body weight.

Getting the Front Wheel Up

To get the front wheel off the ground, you need to preload and punch.

Preload: The preload part is straightforward. Push your weight down into the bike to preload the suspension. This'll give you some rebounding energy that'll help get the wheel up.

Punch: As soon as you're low over the seat, it's time for the punch. As quick as you can, push your feet and arms forward and throw your weight back. You want to keep your arms locked straight so that it's your weight that brings that wheel up rather than pulling the wheel up with your arms.

Keep even pressure on both sides of the handlebar and on both pedals to keep the bike in balance. If you try to lift the bars with just your arms, you'll drop your chest forward, which forces the wheel down.

Balancing

Now that the wheel's up, you can work on holding it there by balancing. It's all in the hips: The key to balancing a manual is in your hips.

- Keep your hips low and over the back wheel, and move them forward and back to stay in balance.
- Keep a finger on the brakes: Keep your finger on the rear brake—if you feel like you're going to tip too far back, all it takes is one tap on the brake, and your front wheel will drop down.

Skill Two: Learn to Bunny Hop

Bunny hops which have to do with lifting both wheels off the ground are an essential skill for getting over rocks, roots, and obstacles without slowing down. When you're practicing your bunny hops, work on each wheel individually.

- Start nice and slow, and draw a line on the ground and work on your timing to make sure both wheels clear it.
- Keep at it and slowly increase your speed until both wheels are in the air at the same time.
- When you've done that, add a small stick and practice clearing that. Once you can clear the stick, take your skills to the trail.

When it comes to performing a bunny hop, you can break down bunny hops into two parts: the front wheel and the back wheel.

FRONT WHEEL

Getting the front wheel off the ground requires similar technique to a manual: preload and punch. Preload down into the bike, and then punch it forward with your arms and legs. The key is to use your weight to get the wheel up.

BACK WHEEL

Spring up and forward:

- As the front wheel is almost to its peak, it's time to get the back wheel off the ground. Your manual has shifted your weight over the rear wheel and preloaded the back of the bike.

- Now quickly spring up and just a little forward. This sudden weight shift will get the rear wheel moving up and off the ground.

Skill Three: Jumping

There's no way around it. Jumps are just plain fun. Once you've been riding for quite a while, you can start hitting small tabletop jumps to get comfortable in the air. All the skills you have from manuals and bunny hops will come in handy, so make sure those are dialed before you start hitting jumps.

Quick Tips to Perfect Jumping

Jumping is of three parts: the takeoff, the air, and the landing.

- ***Takeoff***
- ***Pumping:***

The key to the takeoff is pumping, and that means you're going to press your body weight into the bike through your feet. You want to pump the trail just before the angle of the slope changes, so you accelerate into the jump. Remember to compress from the hips and keep your chest up to leave room for the bike to come through the jump.

- ***SPRING UP:***

As the front wheel is about to leave the ground, start extending your legs and stand up fast. You want your legs to be fully extended as your back wheel hits the lip of the jump, so your bike will come with you into the air. Your pump at the base of the takeoff will preload the bike, so it rebounds off the ground with some force.

TIMING IS KEY:

When it comes to the back wheel, timing is important. If you start to spring up too early before your front wheel is at the lip, you'll waste some of the preload, and you might come up short on your jump. If you extend after the lip, there's nothing for your wheels to push off.

- ***THE AIR***

Stay calm:

Once you're in the air, breathe and relax. If you can stay loose, your bike will stay balanced, your landing will be smoother, and you'll be able to adjust the bike underneath you if you must.

- ***LOOK AHEAD:***

You also want to look ahead to the landing. Find your line and pay special attention to the angle of the slope.

- ***THE LANDING***

Match your tires to the slope:

As you come down, you need to make sure the tires are going to hit at the same time. If you come down with too much weight on either wheel, you could go over the bars or lose control. If it's a steep landing, drop the bars, and scoop the back wheel up.

- ***STRETCH OUT:***

As you're maneuvering the bike, you're also extending your arms and legs so that when you land you can suck up that energy, just like a shock. If you're too low over your bike, you won't be able to absorb that impact energy, and you could lose control.

- ***THE POINT WHERE YOU WANT TO GO:***

Make sure that your front wheel is pointed in the direction you want to go. Even if your landing is a little crooked, if your front wheel is pointed straight, the rest of your bike will follow.

- ***LOOK AHEAD:***

As always make sure to look ahead down the trail. You don't want to land a perfect jump and forget there's another one just ahead.

TOP MOUNTAIN BIKING EXERCISES

Mountain biking is a dynamic sport. It requires full-body engagement to stay balanced, in control and powerful on the bike, so it is important to build strength and several other body skills.

During my training towards completing one of the longest hiking trails in the US, the Pacific Northwest Trail (Montana to Washington), my strength and power on the bike has been a top priority.

With the help of my team, I started performing the following exercises to build strength. The great thing about these exercises is that they require few equipment and can be completed just about anywhere!

SQUAT JUMPS

- Stand with your feet shoulder-width apart.
- Have your hands on your hips to start.
- Sit into the squat – look ahead and keep your back straight.
- Pause and burst up with as much power as you can.
- Land stable with both feet.

PUSH UPS

Push-ups are an upper body exercise that improves upper body strength by working your chest, arms and shoulders.

- Place your hands shoulder-width apart

- Bring your chest as close to the floor as you can without touching it.

- As you return to the starting position, don't lock out your elbows.

- Make sure to look at something a foot in front of you to prevent you from bobbing your head and reaching to the floor with your chin closer to the floor rather than your chest.

Single Dead Lift

Single leg deadlifts emphasize the posterior side of your body by working your glutes, hamstrings, and quads.

- Start off by balancing on one leg then lean forward, making sure to keep your core tight and spine is neutral.

- Stop once your upper body is parallel to the floor.

- Squeeze your glutes and hamstrings on the working leg to get back to the starting position.

Lunges

Lunges are a lower body exercise that works your glutes, hamstrings, and quads.

- Start by making sure that your knee does not pass your toe and that most of your weight is on your front leg.
- Also, make sure you back leg is bent and as you come back up press through your heel.
- Repeat with your other leg when done.
- Throughout this exercise make sure that your chest is out, the core is tight, and spine is neutral.

PLANKS

This exercise strengthens your core and builds endurance in your arms, shoulders, and core muscles.

- Start on your elbows with your spine as straight as possible.
- Hold this position for the desired length of time, and do not twist or sag at the waist.
- If you want to mimic being on a mountain bike, do the plank on your hands, it strengthens the stabilizer muscles in your shoulder joint.
- Perform three sets of 20 repetitions with 30 seconds of rest in-between.
- Hold them for 25 seconds, and then increase your time accordingly.
- To improve endurance, perform the exercise in a quick format — one after another with very little to no rest.

BIKE SAFETY

How to Be Safe on the Bike

Ready to take to your bike to the streets and start road cycling or commuting? We know riding your bike in traffic can be intimidating, but with these tips, you will be on your way to becoming a safer and more confident rider.

Always Ride with a Helmet

Wearing a helmet is smart, not only because it protects your brain (you only get one), but also because most helmets have reflective colors that help you be seen on the road.

Wear Colorful/Reflective Clothing

No, you don't have to rock full spandex on your ride into work. Wear what you feel comfortable in for the length of ride you are doing and the type of bike you are riding on. However, your commute may not be the best time to break out that all-black jumpsuit. Be smart about your clothing choices and know that brighter clothes make you more visible on the road.

Always Ride with Lights, Day or Night.

Lighting up your bike is a good idea any time of day or night. Small flashing lights are easy to use and could help motorists see you.

Perform a Safety Check on Your Bike.

Always check tire pressure, brakes, bolts and make sure your drivetrain is working properly before you head out on your ride. Even though you may only be heading out on a short trip, getting a flat tire due to improper inflation will slow you down, and could cause a safety hazard. Check out our ABC Safety Check to learn how to make sure your bike is safe to ride.

Be prepared!

It is better to be safe than sorry. Here are some items you might be forgetting on your next road ride or commute: Identification, money, a fully charged cell phone, bike lock, sunglasses, sunscreen, extra lights, extra layers of clothing, tube, patch kit, multi-tool, tire levers, and bike pump.

Know the rules of the road.

Be familiar with your local traffic laws. In most cases, you should ride your bike like you are a vehicle and obey all the same traffic laws as a car. However, in some areas laws differ for the cyclist. Know before you go!

Practice, practice, practice!

If you are new to cycling—or have a new bike—get used to riding on neighborhood roads before heading out into busy streets. Get comfortable looking behind you while maintaining a straight path; it is a skill you will often use while riding in traffic.

Learn your local cycling routes.

Let's face it; some roads are just better for cycling than others. Make sure you know your go-to routes, so you don't have to rely on your phone or a map while you are on your way into work or out for a spin. Not only can you avoid the high-traffic areas, but you can also take note of those steep hills!

Learn proper hand signals and use them!

Drivers and other cyclists cannot read your mind. At all times, signal your intent, whether it is to turn right or left, slow or stop.

Move over for parked cars.

You may have to move over into a traffic lane while riding for various reasons—a pothole, loose gravel or pedestrians. Always move over into the traffic lane to give yourself at least 3 feet/ 1 meter between you and a car parked along the street to avoid hitting a car door that suddenly opens.

STAY TO THE RIGHT, BUT NOT OUT OF SIGHT!

When riding with traffic, stay to the right of the lane, but not if it compromises your safety. If the lane is too narrow for a driver to pass safely within the lane, ride more to the center of the lane. This will ensure the driver slows down to pass, without getting too close for comfort. If visibility is compromised because of curving roads, make yourself more visible by riding to the center of the lane.

STAY ALERT, KEEP YOUR COOL AND BE CONFIDENT.

Riding in traffic is not the time to think about what you are going to eat for dinner. Stay alert and never assume a driver sees you on your bike. Make eye contact with drivers when possible. If a driver makes an error and compromises your safety, keep your cool.

Getting angry will only make the situation worse. Pull over to the side of the road, take some time to catch your breath and consider how you might prevent the situation in the future. The best way to stay safe on the road is to ride with confidence.

Conclusion

This chapter introduces you to developing advanced mountain biking skills. We have been able to cover important mountain biking skills such as casing a jump, riding over obstacles, and riding safely.

CHAPTER FIVE: INTRODUCING YOUR KIDS TO MOUNTAIN BIKING- FOR PARENTS

If you're a mountain biking parent, you might be thinking of introducing your kids to mountain biking. It's a great activity to boost confidence, connect with the great outdoors and create a special relationship with your child.

When introducing children to any sport or activity, a thousand questions riddle our minds; how do we introduce our kids to mountain biking in a welcoming environment? How do we ensure their safety and manage elements of risk? What if they aren't interested or can't stand the thought of having their parents teach them a new skill?

To help you along the process of introducing your child to mountain biking, I've put together a list of seven helpful tips to ensure success.

1. Discuss It with Them

It might seem obvious and easy, but it's important to talk to your child. Find out what interests them and if any of their friends might like to try mountain biking with them. It might make it a little easier to have a buddy their own age learns with them. If they don't show an initial interest, don't push it on them.

Plant the seed by talking about all the fantastic things you enjoy about mountain biking; the thrill, the adventure and get them excited. Offer to take them on their first ride, and see if they would prefer a one on one experience or a group bike session with friends.

2. Find A Suitable Bike

Buying a bike that fits your child's height and body structure is of utmost importance, as it will allow them to have more control over the bike. They will be able to enjoy each ride to the fullest and take their riding skills to the next level.

Riding a bike that doesn't fit properly can also be a safety concern, as it's harder to practice proper body positioning and create good habits from the start. Visit your local bike shop and have them test ride a variety of different bikes from different manufacturers. Review sizing charts and make sure your child feels comfortable.

I would also suggest that you include your kid in the buying process as it will make them feel more involved. If you're unsure if your child will enjoy mountain biking, think about renting a bike before committing to a big purchase. Ensure that you have a mountain bike helmet that fits properly and that it offers maximum protection. You may also wish to have other protective equipment such as knee pads, elbow pads, and gloves.

3. Get Started Slowly

The thrill, the rush of adrenaline and immense joy that we get from mountain biking is difficult to describe in words, and yes, we also want our kids to experience the same thing, and they'll get there eventually. Don't get them in over their head right off the bat. Practice body positioning, stance and balance exercises on simple, flat terrain.

Practice on your lawn, or take them to a local park. Grab small objects to use as obstacles (small logs, flat rocks etc.) so they can practice biking over them. Let them ride at their own pace. Get them used to tight turns by using cones (or any object) to create a steering course in the parking lot.

Look up mountain bike youth development programs in your community, they might be interested in doing an afternoon introductory lesson with a coach, as opposed to learning from their parent ;)

4. Start Riding Off-Road

Start with easy trails and keep the rough stuff for later. Broad jeep trails or paved trails in the neighborhood would be ideal for your kid to start their mountain biking career! Moreover, you should let your kid take the lead, if they get tired, take a break. But don't push them too hard. It's all about having fun... sooner or later, they'll most likely by out-biking you!

5. Go Easy on Them

If you want to mountain bike with your child (or any child), patience is key! Offer them encouragement, constructive feedback and celebrate milestones. Instead of finding faults with your child's riding, solve obstacles together. Riding with them will strengthen your bond and make it a memorable experience for both of you.

6. *Facing Difficult Trails*

Don't underestimate their abilities, but ensure you manage elements of risk. Kids are usually fearless and fast learners. It is imperative that you allow them the freedom to make their own decisions and let them find solutions. Don't get mad if they decide to walk a section of trail and ask if they want to see you ride a section first that they are nervous about riding. If needed, get off your bike and walk with them, talk them through difficult obstacles provide a slow progression of more difficult trails.

7. *Technical Riding*

Once they have strong bike handling skills and feel confident on beginner and intermediate trails, it's time to teach them some more advanced skills and recognize that you might not be the best teacher! Technical climbing, rolls downs, small jumps and drop need to be taught in a progression.

Start small, practice (a lot!) and session sections of the trail. at this point, you'll have a good idea how interested your child is in mountain biking and if they'd like to continue recreationally, try racing or join a skill throughout the clinic. which brings us back to #1... talk to them! it's important to know where they're at entire learning process, and what they hope to get out of their biking experience.

10 TIPS FOR GROUP MOUNTAIN BIKE RIDES

Group mountain bike rides are an amazing way to meet new people, learn new skills and discover new trails. Mountain bike club rides or organizing a group of friends to bike together offers up a completely different experience than riding on your own.

When riding in groups, you may be more likely to push your limits and try different line choices as you'll feed off the skills and motivation from other riders. Whether you're learning from riders in the group or teaching riders, you'll be improving your skills along the way.

To get the most out of your group ride and ensure everyone has a positive experience, you should become familiar with the following group ride tips. Whether it's a group of friends or a club ride where you don't know anyone, it's important to review the following before setting out on the trail.

1. Agree on A Route

Talk to your fellow riding buddies before leaving the trailhead. Agree on a preferred route and create a game plan. Consider everyone's skill level, knowledge of the area, trail conditions, how long everyone would like to ride for and what trails the most novice rider in the group would be comfortable riding.

2. Be Prepared

Make sure all riders are self-sufficient or that there are a couple designated riders that can assist with trailside maintenance issues. To avoid maintenance issues, do a bike check before leaving the trailhead and have each rider check the following:

- check the tire pressure
- check the quick release skewers to make sure they are locked
- test the brakes
- lube the chain

- check the shifting

Ensure all riders have the appropriate safety gear to ride and have the basic tools to fix a flat tire or a broken chain. Here is a basic list of items each rider should have:

- water
- trailside snack
- spare tube, patch kit
- hand pump
- multi-tool with chain breaker
- chain lube
- tire lever
- spare derailleur hanger (especially for longer rides)

3. *It's Not A Race*

Ok, depending on the group... maybe you want to race! There will always be faster riders and slower riders. It's important to respect and manage different paces appropriately to make sure everyone has a great riding experience. After all, it's not a group ride if the fastest rider speeds ahead all the time and doesn't wait to regroup.

Identify stopping points along the trail for group members to reconvene. Plus, the moments when riders come together are usually the best - it gives people an opportunity to talk about the section of trail they just ride, laugh at their near-miss wipe-outs and pump each other up for what's ahead.

4. *Leave Space*

Nobody likes it when another rider rides their back wheel. Leave enough space between each rider so people can stop safely if the person in front of them crashes or stops suddenly.

5. Stop and Plan

Group rides are an amazing way to improve your skills. If there is a section of trail you've always struggled with ask for pointers from riders that can clean it. Watch other riders tackle the obstacle, and consider their body position and line choice. Then, try it and ask for feedback!

6. Trail Etiquette

When riding in large groups, it's important to practice proper trail etiquette and be respectful of other riders and trail users. Follow these tips:

- Respect trail closures
- Leave no trace
- Control your bike
- Don't scare animals
- Yield appropriately

If you're descending, yield to riders that are climbing. Yield to all other trail users (hikers, horseback riders).

- Anticipate other riders when going around corners.

7. WATCH FOR FORKS

Keep the group together and watch for forks in the trail. In general, try to have the first rider wait at forks and allow time for the group to reconvene. If riders don't want to wait, make sure each rider calls out "LEFT" or "RIGHT" to inform the rider behind them which way to go. The rider behind should call out "OK" to communicate they know which way to go, and then pass the message onto the person behind them. Fingers crossed it doesn't turn into a game of broken telephone! Ultimately, your goal is to leave no one behind!

8. Know Your Limits

Thanks to the motivation of other riders, it's easy to push yourself on group rides and step out of your comfort zone. At the same time, be sure to recognize your limits and only push yourself so far.

9. Check In

Throughout the ride, be sure to check in with your fellow riders. If you notice someone falling behind, wait for them to ensure they still have a little fuel in their tank to finish the ride. We all have off days and excel in different areas. It's always a great feeling to be motivated by other group members.

10. Celebrate

Perhaps the best part of riding with a group of friends is the post-ride chats, jokes and beverages. Mountain biking brings people together and creates a rock-solid community of people who want to share their passion for two-wheeled adventures. It's time to hold your post-ride beer up high and cheers to the ride, and the moments you'll never forget.

HOW TO *PREVENT* A FLAT TIRE

Nothing is 100% effective in preventing you from getting a flat tire on your bike. You do; however, you have several options that can greatly reduce your likelihood of getting a flat. With this advice and/or products, you may never need to fuss with tube punctures or patch kits again.

TIRE PRESSURE

Your first strategy should always be to make sure you are riding with the proper tire pressure.

Each tire has a preferred air-pressure range, which is measured in psi (pounds per square inch). Look on the tire sidewall for the recommended pressure. As a rule:

- Road tires should run between 100 to 140 psi.
- Mountain bike tires should run between 30 to 50 psi.
- Urban and casual bike tire should run between 60 and 80 psi.

Under-inflation can lead to problems with "pinch flats." This can occur when you hit a bump and your under-inflated tire compresses all the way to the rim, causing 2 small holes that resemble a snake bite. Over-inflation, on the other hand, doesn't cause flats although it's possible to blow out the tube in extreme cases.

Use a tire pump or gauge to check your pressure. Higher-end tire pumps will include a psi gauge, but if you have a lower-end pump, you'll need to carry your own tire pressure gauge. Be sure to know whether you have a Presta or Schrader valve stem (the slimmer Presta valve needs to have the top nut unscrewed before checking pressure).

Basic Tire Care

It's a good idea to periodically inspect your bike tires for embedded glass, rock shards or other sharp objects, especially after riding a route that has substantial debris. These small embedded items may not cause an immediate flat but can slowly work their way through a tire to eventually cause a puncture. Use your fingernail or a small tool to remove this debris before it causes a problem.

Periodically check your tire sidewalls and tread for excessive wear, damage, dryness or cracking. Tires with any of these symptoms increase your risk for a flat tire. If unsure about their condition, ask a bike pro at your local REI or other reputable bike shop to evaluate your tires.

Tube Sealants

This option is handy because you can repair an existing flat tire with it or use it as a preventive measure to avoid future flats. The concept is simple: Squeeze in a bit of sealant through the valve stem to coat the inside of the tube. In the case of a small puncture or cut, the sealant quickly fills the leak and creates a plug that often outlasts the tube or the tire around it.

You can make use of the REI sealant which are of two types. The Slime brand is designed to be injected directly into Schrader-type tubes only; the Café Latex brand is designed to be injected into Presta-type tubes or tubeless tires. Café Latex requires use of a no-mess injector which is sold separately.

Some tubes (with both Schrader and Presta valves) come "pre-Slimed" to offer a preventive approach to flat tires. These tubes are typically a thicker thorn-resistant variety, that when pre-injected with Slime, offer an excellent flat-avoidance strategy.

The downsides to sealants? Some can be a little messy to install, and sealants alone do not protect against large gashes or cuts.

Tire Liners

A tire liner is a thin strip of extruded-plastic that fits between the tire and the tube. This extra layer greatly reduces the chance of puncture flats from thorns, glass or other sharp objects. Liners are popular and work well, but they do add 6 oz. or more to the weight of your tires which adds noticeably to your rolling resistance in higher performance tires. However, if you live in an area with lots of thorns or road debris, liners could be well worth the weight.

Puncture-Resistant Tires and Tubes

Another option is to change out your tires to ones specifically designed to resist flats. These tires won't feel as speedy as standard bike tires, but bike-commuting customers have told us that they experience flats much less frequently when using them.

How do they work? Many tires makers employ a durable belt of aramid fibers (such as the well-known Kevlar® brand) to resist punctures; others simply increase the tread thickness. These tires are marketed by a variety of proprietary names: the Serfas Flat Protection System, the Continental Safety System, the Michelin ProTek reinforcement system and so on. The downside of these tires is that they are relatively heavy which reduces your pedaling efficiency.

Finally, consider using thorn-resistant tubes. They are simply thicker (and heavier) versions of conventional tubes

SIMPLE DO-IT-YOURSELF (DIY) TIPS TO FIX COMMON BIKE NOISES

Bike noises such as creaks, squeaks, squeals and clicks are more than just annoying when you're riding your bike: they may indicate a serious problem that, left unfixed, could result in injury to you and/or damage to your bike.

Finding where noises originate can sometimes be difficult. Try your best to identify where you think the noise is coming from, then attempt to eliminate the problem.

Diagnosing and repairing the most common bike noises requires beginner to intermediate knowledge of bike parts and how they work. If you're not sure how to fix something, take your bike to your local shop for service.

How to Fix Bike Chain Noises

A squeaky chain needs to be lubed. Do this by placing the bike in a stand or by leaning it against a wall with the drivetrain facing you so that the pedals can spin freely. Drip a drop of lube on each chain link as you pedal backwards with your hand. Continue to pedal backwards to work in the lube.

Before your next ride, wipe off any excess lube with a clean rag using the same positioning and backwards pedaling.

If your chain is severely rusty or has stiff links, take it to a bike shop to have the chain replaced.

How to Fix a Clicking Chain

A clicking noise often comes from your chain wanting to jump up or down a gear on the rear cassette. This can typically be fixed by adjusting the tension of the cable that runs from your shifter to your rear derailleur. Depending on the style of your bike, there will be barrel adjusters located on the shifters, cables and/or near the rear derailleur. Use the barrel adjusters to fine-tune the cable tension.

Turn the barrel adjuster ¼ turn at a time. Turn the adjusters clockwise if the chain seems to want to fall into a smaller cog. Turn the barrel adjuster counter-clockwise if the chain won't shift up to the larger cog.

If you've turned the barrel adjuster more than a full turn and it hasn't solved the problem, see a bike technician. The clicking could be caused by a bent derailleur hanger.

How to Fix Squeaky Bike Brakes

Squeaking brakes are one of the few squeaks that you don't fix with lube. Never lube your brakes.

First, check if your wheel is properly attached: Before attempting to silence a squeak, make sure your wheel is properly seated in the dropout of your front fork or rear part of the frame. A wheel that is not seated properly will be off-kilter and may rub against one brake pad or part of the frame.

Next, check if your wheel is true: To make sure your wheel is true (not wobbling side to side), put your bike in a stand or lift the squeaky wheel off the ground and spin the wheel.

If you have rim brakes, watch the rim and the brake pads. If you see wobble or inconsistent rubbing between the rim and brake pads, your wheel needs truing.

If you have disc brakes, watch the rotor and brake pads. If you see wobbling and rubbing, either your wheel needs truing or you may have a bent rotor.

If your wheel needs truing, or you have a bent rotor, take your bike to the shop. If your wheel is true, you can proceed to the next steps.

Check for dirt and wear: Try cleaning the pads and rim or rotor with rubbing alcohol or a cleaner designed specifically for brakes. Then rough the pads and rotor lightly with sandpaper (with disc brakes, it will be easiest if you remove the pads from the calipers before sanding them).

Then, check that your brake pads haven't worn down too much. There needs to be enough pad that the metal piece that holds the pads won't touch your rim or rotor.

Most pads for rim brakes have markings to show when they need to be replaced.

Check disc brake pads by removing the wheel and looking into the space where the rotor spins, or by removing the pads themselves. As a general guideline, disc brake pads should be replaced if the pad thickness, including the metal holder, is less than 3mm. Be careful not to squeeze the brake lever when the wheel is off.

Check the alignment of your rim brake pads: If your rim brake pads are hitting the rim flat, that will make them squeak when you're braking. Reposition them using a hex wrench so that the front of each pad contacts the rim slightly before the rear of each pad. This is called toeing the pads in.

Whether you have disc brakes or rim brakes, if your brake pads are off-center, it's best to take your bike to a shop to have them adjusted. Off-center brakes cause one side of the brakes to make contact with the rotor or rim before the other one does, resulting in poor braking power.

How to Fix Rear-Suspension Pivot Noises

The rear suspension on a mountain bike has multiple pivot points that can develop squeaks when they're loose or dry, or when the bearings need to be replaced.

Check if the pivots are tight using the appropriate size hex wrench for the pivot bolts. Pivot bolts should be tightened to the bike manufacturer's specifications using a torque wrench.

Drip lube into the joint between the pivot and the frame. Check for play by grasping the internal piece of the pivot and wiggling it side to side. If lube and tightening don't solve the squeak, take your bike in for service.

How to Fix a Squeaky Bike Suspension

If your front shock is squeaking, you may have it accidently locked out when you're riding technical terrain. This can cause a sneeze-like squeak. Open your shock to the ride position on technical terrain to eliminate the noise.

How to Fix a Clunking Bike Suspension

If your front shock is clunking, you may need to add pressure to it. If these solutions don't solve the problem, or if your shock is leaking a significant amount of oil, take your bike in for service.

How to Fix a Squeaky Bike Saddle

Usually squeaks coming from your saddle indicate that the saddle clamp that attaches to the rails of your saddle needs to be tightened. Look under your saddle to determine how it attaches—with one or two bolts on the fore and/or aft sides of your seat post or on the side(s).

Using a hex wrench or star-shaped torx wrench—whichever is compatible with your saddle bolt(s)—tighten the bolt or bolts to eliminate any movement.

Also confirm that the saddle clamp is within the fore and aft limits of the seat. Most saddles have marks on the rails that show maximum forward and rear positions.

If your saddle is tight but it tips forward or backward, or if it continues to squeak, see a bike mechanic. You may have a worn or defective saddle clamp, or your saddle may need to be replaced.

How to Fix a Creaky Bike Seat Post

If a creak is coming from your seat post, not your saddle, it likely needs lube. If your seat post is aluminum, remove it by loosening the bolt at the seat collar and wipe off any grease and grit. Then, apply a light coating of paste grease with your finger and put the post back in your bike frame. If your post is carbon, use a carbon fiber paste, not grease.

How to Fix a Squeaky Bike Crank

The most common cause of a squeaky crank is that the bolt is loose. Check for play in your cranks by pulling on one side and trying to wiggle it side to side. If there is play, check that your crank bolts are tight using a hex wrench—bolts should be hand-tight.

If tightening the bolt doesn't eliminate the squeak, or if you have play even when the bolts are tight, have your bike serviced at a shop.

How to Fix a Squeaky Bike Derailleur

Dry pulley wheels can cause your rear derailleur to squeak. First clean them with a pre-moistened bike-specific cleaning towel or diluted citrus cleaner and a rag and/or cleaning brush—a toothbrush works great. Use a drop of lube on the axis of each pulley wheel, then spin the pedals to turn the wheels and work in the lube. Also place a drop of lube on the hinges of the front and/or rear derailleur to keep parts moving freely.

How to Fix a Rattling Bike Headset

Headset bolts can loosen over time, resulting in wobbly steering and rattling noise. Check for a loose headset by placing your bike on the ground, engaging the front brake and rocking the bike front to back. If you feel a clunking, you may have a loose headset.

Step 1: Using a hex wrench, loosen the two horizontal pinch bolts on your stem.

Step 2: Gently tighten the headset cap bolt. If you tighten it too much, you'll feel resistance when you turn your handlebars side to side and may notice a squeaking noise when you ride. Once you have the right tension, retighten the side bolts.

Then, with the bike on the ground, sandwich your front wheel between your legs and aggressively try to turn the handlebars side to side. If they move independently of the wheel, you need to re-loosen the side bolts and retighten the center bolt.

Be aware that clunking in bikes with front suspension can be caused by bushings in the suspension rather than a loose headset. If you follow the steps above and still feel clunking, take your bike to a qualified bike tech for a thorough inspection.

How to Fix Creaky Bike Pedals

Place a drop of lube on your pedal springs and at the joint in the spindle. Wipe off excess lube. If your pedals are grinding or stiff, you may need your bearings serviced at your local bike shop.

If lubing the pedal springs doesn't eliminate the creaking, check to make sure the cleats on your bike shoes are tight. Loose cleats can cause creaking.

How to Fix Creaky Bike Handlebars

If you have any up and down play and creaking in your handlebar, you need to tighten your stem bolts. With the front wheel between your legs, or the bike in a stand, use a hex wrench to hand tighten the four bolts at the center of your handlebar where it attaches to the stem. Check that top and bottom and left and right bolts are all tightened roughly evenly.

If this solution doesn't eliminate the creak, have your bike checked out by a qualified bike technician. It's possible the creaking is caused by a crack.

How to Fix Squeaky Bike Brake Levers and Shift Levers

If your shift or brake levers are squeaking, add a drop of lube to the cable—accessible when the brake lever is engaged, or when the shift lever is pressed.

How to Fix Rattling Bolts

Bikes have lots of bolts and any one of them can work loose and rattle while you're riding. If you hear rattling, try to locate where it's coming from and make sure all bolts in that area are snug. Be sure to check the bolts that hold your bottle cage to your bike frame. A loose bottle cage can make a lot of noise.

General Bike Maintenance Advice

Get your bike serviced annually at your local bike repair shop. A qualified bike mechanic will address clicks, creaks and squeaks before they become a problem.

Keep your bike clean and well lubed to help reduce wear and tear and squeaks and creaks. Keep a tube or tub of paste grease on hand, as well as a bottle of liquid lube suited for the conditions where you ride. Always use bike-specific lubes and cleaners.

The only way to make sure all the bolts on your bike are tightened to manufacturers' specifications is to use a torque wrench. How tight bolts should be is often noted right next to the bolt, whether it's on your rotor or your stem. Set the recommended torque on the wrench, tighten the bolt and when the proper tightness is achieved the wrench will release pressure. Don't confuse an adjustable torque wrench with a torx wrench, which is a star-shaped bit wrench.

CONCLUSION

This chapter introduces various maintenance tips that is needed to enjoy your mountain biking journeys. We have been able to cover important mountain biking maintenance tips. We believe that consistent practice is the key to succeeding as a mountain biker.

ACKNOWLEDGEMENTS

I'm grateful for everyone who took a chance on me, especially in the early days. From the contributors at REI.com, Sacred Rides, MTB Forums, and other Pro Mountain Biking Bloggers who gave me permission to use their material.

I also want to thank every mountain biking parents instilling the mountain biking culture in their kids, I really want to say a big kudos. For all the kids pushing and chasing their Mountain biking dream, I would love to encourage you to keep dreaming and training. In the words of my beloved father, if you can picture it, you can feature in it.

Thanks to everyone who was kind enough to assist me in the writing, structuring of contents, editing, and sharing of ideas, you guys are great! I am extremely honored. Thanks to the people who I've met up with in my mountain biking journey so far, I'm really excited about meeting many more people over the next couple of years.

MOUNTAIN
BIKING for kids
Mindset Development Guide
Christopher C. Keller

Made in the USA
San Bernardino, CA
06 June 2020